The Creation Of OG

Urban Organics Organic Green

By Magdalene Beckett

Published By Andrea Spruill

The Creation of OG:
Urban Organics of Organic Greens

Written By Magdalene Beckett
Published By Andrea Spruill

ISBN: 978-1-7-323770-8-0

" EXCERPT"

"My name is Andrea Spruill.
I know my last name don't fit me shade or my grade. I've known this my whole life,
I've gotten in to many fights…. So many that I wear my fights like stripes.
Yet, later on in life that last name "Spruill" provided job Opportunities at least until I walked in to the room,
Night Dark, Bright smile, Curves for miles.
"Yes I'm the Gods Child"
I thought as I smiled.
But yet, deep down I felt the frown as thy face drop down. When my melon enters the room before me the cries of my ancestors as they drop to their knees, I hear the screams and pleads don't give in,
Yet the demeanor of the employer say's not this job today,No way.
But In my Mind and my physical I feel no shame. I slam down my resume with the present that Nope I'm here to stay. See in my mind I paid for an education and not a reflection of Rejection due to my complexion. See Education can be a crazy weapon. An Intellectual perception with tight vocabulary that floats off my lips like feathers and tough like leather. Weather you know or not I've seen the idea of your plot. See I was told my soul and body is all I got. The true temple is in your temple your brain when educated is insane. Not Plain nor surly not something that holds shame no that's not me. I proclaim that I am not my last name. Because I know my last

name is not my claim to fame. And I holds No shame! Do You Know Me?
Andrea is Who I am and who I be!

By
The Publisher
Andrea Spruill

Acknowledgements:

This book is dedicated to my family, who stood by me through all my
ventures. To the ones who never judge me yet supported me. To my future
family keep your head up, and strive to achieve every dream. You can only
fail if you don't try. No excuses, No regrets

Preface

This book was developed because I am tired of people Buying garbage and calling it cannabis, including me. I have brought some real crap in my life. Buying crap weed has harmed me more than helped me. People who smoke cannabis or eat edibles do so for a reason. Cannabis has many medical properties that help with anxiety, pain, and seizures just to name a few. We don't need to poison ourselves for someone else's profit! Grow Your Own. This book is a guide on How to do just that!!!!

By Magdalene Beckett

Contents

Forward

A little back story of the creation of O.G – O.G stands for original green. Green that is grown without manipulation of water, sun or soil. You ever wonder why when you smoke bud and get a dry throat? Maybe you get a slight headache temporary loss of your taste buds? Or a cough with a fluid that you can't expel? Do you know how your weed is being grown and cured? No, you just purchase and smoke, right. Most people experience these symptoms and don't equate it to the bud their ingesting in their body. Ever google how to grow weed?

There are several hundreds of videos on how to grow weed. These videos will teach you how to infuse your soil with chemicals to increase yield,videos on how to control PH levels of the dirt. What nutrients to buy to infuse into the water to make your bud flower quicker. They tell you how to manipulate light to trick the natural process of the maturing of your bud plant. Its amazing, crazy and super complicated. If you continue to research, you will also realize that they change the most important part which is the curing. There are videos that teach you to dehydrate your bud for quick dry. Also to spray your buds with chemicals to make it more potent or make it smell more potent. Sometimes they even add more additives drugs to the bud. Can you believe that! Its true—Google It! That is why this book was developed.

This is a short- straight to the point read with no frills. Times are changing and if you're going to smoke you need to grow your own plant. With purchasing from anyone or company you risk manipulation of your bud. One plant of OG can yield anywhere from ½ pound to a pound of weed. That is plenty for a single smoker and the savings from growing your own will allow you to free up money. The creation of this handbook is to ease you into the world of growing your own natural weed, without any chemicals or crazy lights or special soils. I hope this can be your guide into this brave new world.

 As mentioned above this will be a no frills look into growing your own weed. This book was written from the experience of trying different methods. This book will teach you how to grow weed in a pot as well as outdoors. I am not a seed expert. The seeds used came from all types—reggie to exotic. I do not know how to tell female seeds from males seeds, sorry, I've tried. There are several videos out there that try to explain how. It has been learned that a male or two isn't bad. Why you ask, males roots makes hemp. Included in this book are recipe for brownies and cannabis butter veg/reg, as well as making use of the entire plant, not just the bud. Without further delay. Let's get into it.

Chapter 1: The Veggie State

The vegetative state. First decide where to put your plant. Will you start in the ground? Will you start in a pot then put it in the ground? Will it be a pot plant? Starting in a pot is way different from starting it in the ground. The sun rises in the east and sets in the west, so if you have a pot plant then chasing the rotation of the sun will become routine. Outside in the ground, among the elements the ground plant will adjust. Pot life is different in a number of ways. Start the plant in a medium pot (some do a seed in a shot glass), but you risk shocking the plant when you transport the plants. Starting in a small environment may cause the plant to not be strong enough to survive the transfer. So use a cup size and put three to four seeds in. Not knowing the sex of the seeds planting four will give you a fifty fifty chance two out of four are girls (fingers crossed). You can start your pot plants at anytime if you want to place them outside you can take them out in early May , but make sure to keep them in the house until then. Pot Life is a longer process verse outside ground life. Make sure they are well drained pots.

Ground Life is much easier for growing but surely more work and risk! When starting your planning in a plot outside be mindful of your neighbors, who may not appreciate 6 foot stalks of weed in their view. Also, you need to plant aromatic herbs or flowers to help conceal the smell of the growth of your bud plant. An earthworm or two can can help with soil retention. Of course all these aren't necessary but can help in the long run. Late May is a great time to turn over the ground and disturb the worms. You can put about 10 healthy looking seeds in the ground pushing them a half a finger deep and cover. At least half will be males. Pull all unwanted weeds strays , chop them up and use them as fertilizer. If the ground is hard and dry after adding the fertilizer of surrounding weeds choppings give the area water. *Note During the winter you can make homemade fertilizer from food scraps like coffee grounds, eggshells, banana peels, orange peels, lemon peels,and apple cords mixed with dirt. There are many more things that you can add to it. Keep in a tight lid container because as it decays it will stink. You can add this mixture to your pot life dirt or the ground dirt it will help them both.*

After a week or two you will start to see your plant break ground and pop up with leaves. It will be a beautiful sight. At this point outside ground plants should be tended to, no unwanted growth should be cleared. Outdoor plants should be regularly watered when there is no rainfall.

Living the Pot Life

Breaking Dirt: You should see something start to break dirt in you pot between 6 and 10 days, give or take a day. In the beginning plant will be a little slower to grow. When your growing in the house you get to really watch the process of the plant take place.

Once it breaks through the dirt it will be smelling like bud. It will grow in height almost every three days or so.

Week 3-5

Pot life is visibly different from ground life. Keeping your pot moist is important. Taking it outside is good to maximize the sun and heat intake, but watch hydration. Pot plant dry out quick and leaves will wilt and turn yellow quickly, be mindful. On days over 90 degrees fahrenheit water moisture of plant is important do not let dry out.

After 30 days I usually sprinkle some eggshells on the top of the soil of the pot, it seems to keep the soil warm and moist. About 30 days your growth in ground plants will begin to get some real height, maybe about a foot or so from the ground. House plants will grow much slower and smaller. Every week you should be clearing the ground of unwanted growth and recycling it as mulch.

You should trim fan leaves off of the plant to send nutrients back to the steam. Don't bald the plant just a few every week.
To Trim Finger leaves take scissors and cut at the base of the leaf

Chapter 2: The Flowering State

Six weeks in and OMG, do you smell that? That shit is all yours! Now it's time to bring out the magnifying glass and at this point you might be able to tell if you have any boy or girl plants. But if you can't don't worry it will come in time. Just keep your ground clear. You should have no unwanted growth around your plant.

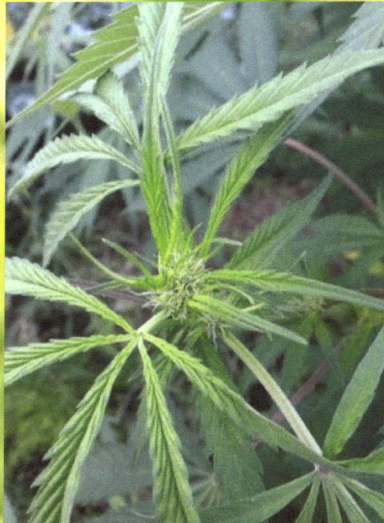

*Note If you didn't hand pick you seeds, odds are so/so that you have male and female plants. Male plants have oval shape that grow close to the stem. Male plants sacks grow into flowers and they can pollinate the female making the female grow seeds. The longer they are exposed to each other the more seeds the female plant will reproduce and it will produce less bud. Female plants produce bud and seeds. The only time females don't produce seeds is if they are not exposed to male plants at all. In this case you only have hand picked female seeds. If you find males

Kill Them!!

At 4-6 weeks

In the four to six weeks of growth all the males should be identified and removed. You are in a very leafy stage right now. Be patient and wait for it. Trimming finger leaves and keeping it short (out of sight) is extremely important. Don't Forget your herbs you grew to curve the smell of the bud plant. Make sure you are tending to them so they do not grow out of control and take over the area. Herbs are good for that.. Harvest some of your planted aroma plant leaves and spread them at the base of your marijuana plant. This will help curve the smell of the marijuana plant. You might also need to add some dirt around the base of your plants. Even before budding or flowering your plant will develop its smell, this smell will only increase. Especially as the temperature rises. So get the herbs like Lavender, thyme, rosemary, and stronger herbs.

Your lady plant should start showing little signs of flowering small buds with some white strains should be visible. Do not get happy and start cutting. Instead check your ground. Make sure the ground is clear. Make sure the base has good dirt and your watering the ground. DO not water the whole plant.

Flowering of ground plant

Water the base of the plant. Watering the whole plant while it is flowering can cause mold on your bud. At this point after rain storms and dewy morning you want to lightly shake each plant to shake off excess water that was not released from the wind blowing. You will want to remove large finger leaves to allow the nutrients to the bud. You plant might even continue to grow in height and produce little buds. Don't get greedy keep your plant short and out of sight.

10 weeks of ground life

It's a sight to see right? You getting all tingaling like buzz by their glising flower. Hopefully being down played by the smell of flourishing herbs nearby. Remove large leaves that surround the bud. The white pistons will start filling out. Some have already started to change colors as leaves in the fall. Your bud white strings should start turning goldish amber or pinkish.

Pot life 8 weeks

Pot life, at this time your baby will just start to show if it is male or female. Pots take longer when in the house. It also can become temperamental. It's found that the longer the plant remains in the house it adapts to the house. So when you move it outside it may not do well. SO pay close attention to see how it reacts to being outside. This seems to be moving a bit slower but if your pot plants has adapted to the outside make sure the pot is drainable, meaning you want any rain water to run right through not flood the pot. This can happen very quickly so keep an eye out and bring all the pots plants inside during drenching rain storms. Some pot plants will not recover from drowning. This is very important and drowning the plant drowns the worms. Oh, did I tell you to find some worms to keep your pot plant happy? Yes, if you can find a worm or two drop them in the pot. Some of the pot plant stems may lean to the side. To prevent that simply put a wooden stick next to them in the pot and tie the steam to the stick or lean them against the stick until the stems thicken, You might what even want to add a little dirt to the pot. As the plant grow add dirt to the base of the stem to keep it covered what the watering will expose. Lightly shift dirt to keep it around the plant.

Pot life week 10

Your stems should still be thin but with a little more stability to them. At this time you should transfer it (your plant) into a larger pot. For this it's found to be easier to let the dirt be dry around the plant. Gently tap around the side of your pot so that it will release as a whole. Prep new pot with dirt at the base. Carefully loosen dirt around base of the planets to loosen the root. Sit on the drt in a new pit. As you sit the plant in lossen the

dirt around the plant then fill in pot with more dirt, water and let it settle. The less you disturb it the less likely it will go into shock.

Ground life week 12

Your plant should look like mini trees between thigh high to waist high. A beautiful sight to see. The smell is amazing and very tempting to taste. Trim the fan leaves. Cut the leaves at the base of his fingers. The leaves are large and dark green. As you collect your leaves you can dry them in a dark place. I drop them in brown paper bags, it works well with drying them and keeping them from molding. Keep the ground clear from wild weeds that grow uninvited they will drain the plants of energy and nutrients. You might even want to chop them up carefully and return to the ground as mulch. Mulch will help to keep the ground moist. It will not dry out as quick with mulch mixed in or on top of the ground. Now if

you did research you would think that it should be budding right now and it might just be a little. Since your growth is chemical free green your plants will not look like what you have seen on the internet. It will be green and luscious. You might have white pistons and small flowers growing. You will also see small leaves growing tightly around the flower. If you don't have flowers yet, no worries. Organic weed is a little slower to grow but will grow.

 *Note Remember that adding chemically altering nutrients will produce flowers quicker, but at the risk of your health. Slow stroll it. Trust that flowering is around the corner. Take the leaves you have dried and put them in a mason jar, they will cure within days and make it a smooth

smoke. They are less potent than bud, but will give you a smooth mellow buzz to stop you from buying suspect bud until yours come to harvest.

Chapter 2: The Flowering State

I know that it's a tearjerker, the smell is so potent you get a little high when up stand up close, I know, I know be patient

16 weeks

Yes you see them, flowers, they are pretty right? Welcome to the flowering stage. Note even though you are flowering the plant will still grow in height. Being mindful of your surrounding keep them to a secluded size where no one can see them. Don't worry about cutting them down. I know I was. Completely scared they would go in shock stop growing and straight up die. Guess what they don't They actually start to bud strong and tighten up. They will produce more buds on the remaining branches. After this time you will surely know if you have any remaining males. If so pull them by the root. Males can still be valuable. Their leaves are smokeable once cured. Roots can be dried and turned into hemp. Hopefully you killed them off early so your flowers are not seeding.

Once you tend to the grown of unwanted wild weeds, break up and return to the ground. You can always add some dirt. When it rains it disturbs the dirt and it can wash away to somewhere else or sink around the plant. Gather up some dirt and fill it in. Make sure your plants are getting water try not to water the flower. Water the ground. By this time you should visit your plant offer at least in the morning to shake off any dew that sits on the bud. You don't want mold to develop so lightly shake each plant.

Your plant has nice flowers aka bud. Your plant has a lot more growing to do. Some of your flowers are developing color to its strains. Some of the pistons will be turning orange or reddish orange. Your stalk are nice and strong. Buds will start to develop up and down the stalk. Be patient don't start harvesting early harvest will mess with

potency of the flower.

Chapter 3: The Pruning State

Week 20

Now is the time when tears are literally in your eyes as the smell is so potent your eyes sort of burn, maybe from the THC or just the beauty of the large buds at the top of the plant soaking up all the sun from sunrise to sunset. It's time to go in and hand harvest. With small scissor, go in and trim a few stalks off the top that are full with colorful fat buds tightly surrounded with sugar leaves. This allow the young bud to be in the sun and push nutrients back down into the plant. The plant will continue to produce new bud and branches reaching towards the sun.

Pruning and trimming the right way will determine how well your bud cures. If you leave too many leaves around the bud it will take longer to dry. It may regain moisture if left with the bud causing mold. So trim as close as possible! For Bud Sake!!

Week 20: Pot life

You will have fan leaves but they will not be as big as the leaves on your outside plant. Remember that you pot plant will grow slower than your ground plants. By this time your plant will have taken to the new pot and should have grown a bit since the moving between the pots. You can take off a few fan leaves but even if bud has starts to develop leave them be. The bud/flower on your pot plant will develop at the top of the plant down. Males will develop sacks and form into flowers if not removed before maturity.

The top branches will start to hang because they are heavy with bud. These are the branches/bud you prune first. If you do not trim the heavy branches they will snap. If they snap it will stop that branch from growing and providing nutrients to the rest of that stem this can cause

your bud on that stem to dry up and or mold up. You will trim them up to where the bud is not colored. Cut the branch on an angle. This allow the branch to heal, itself and not just die. It will continue to provide the remaining flowing strength and nutrients. The remaining bud/flower with continue to mature and get its color. The bud you trimed needs all leaves removed from the stem and to be put in a place to dry. Preferably a brown paper bag. This will allow the leaves to dry. Also the leaves will retain their green color and potency. Believe it or not, curing leaves can be used to smoke or make edibles with.

Drying and Pruning

This process is the most important part of preserving and curing your bud. You must remove the large leaves-- save them! Then bag them in a brown paper bag. The leaves that are the closest to the flower/bud are very special. These are sugar leaves. The sugar leaves should be kept separate these are great for making butter. Trim the leaves off as close to the bud as possible. Leave the bud on the stem, hang the stem upside down in a dark dry place at least at 65-70 F if it is very humid at add a fan to even air out. If you remove the bud from the stem spread bud out and let dry on a brown paper bag in the same temperature.

Bud on stem can take anywhere from four to seven days to dry completely you must make sure it is dry but not crunchy. When it is dry place in a mason jar. If you have over dried place a undried bud in the jar for 24 hours then remove, bud will have soften. You must open and air the bud once a day for the first seven day this is important. Some bud will

re- moisturize itself if not aired and will mold not cure.

Pot Life

You pot plant should be budding/flowering by now. The top of the plant is heavy and probably leaning to the side. Gently investigate the steam to see where bud/flower has gaining color and maturity to the flower. Place sticks next to the plant for support. If the flower or bud has gained its gold or reddish orange color the bud cut the mature bud only. If your plant is healthy it will continue to grow and mature bud/flower still left on the stem. Trim large leaves but not to many.

Pot plants are a little different about their leaves then ground plant. Make sure you are still providing water to your plant. Also make sure it's either outside or in a window getting max sun.

Chapter 4: The Harvesting State

Harvesting can be a bit tricky your going to end up with some young bud/flowers. Only because a healthy plant doesn't stop producing. It will continue to grow as long as it hot enough. So stagger your harvest start cutting from the top. Sometimes the sides branches will continue to stretch out so that the bud can get a much sun as possible.They will also be heavy so they will start to drop but not in a sickly way. It will clearly be dropping because its heavy. Don't get upset heavy is very good sign that you plant is healthy and full of bud. You must cut the branches that are heavy first. If you don't the branch will break. If it break it will send shock to the stem stopping growth and nutrient to other bud and

branches. This is bad. So be very choosy as to where and when to cut. First It's not recommend chopping down the whole plant at one time. One you do it will be an abundance to clean cut up and dry at one time. This will create a lot of problems. TRUST. Staggering will allow you to control moisture. The more bud you dry at one time the more moisture will be in air. Moisture creates mold on flowers very quickly and will not be reversible.

Chapter 5: The Drying State

You should pre plan a place that stays dark. This place should be a place that stays dry and cool. The temperature should be able to stay between 65-70 degrees. You should also have a supply of mason jars with sealable lids to retain freshness. This jars should be clean. The area in which you choose to dry your flower in should be clear of clutter. It should have a place to put a fan just incase temperatures fluctuate. There are several way to dry your flower. Here are three methods to dry your bud/flower successfully.

Method 1

You will need Brown twine. The type you would wrap around herbs. No plastic. You will need this for two of the methods. You can use a hanger and tie the end of the stem to it hanging it upside down. This allows the opinid or THC to pull into the flower and away from the stem. You will notice that if you remove the thinner stems from the larger stems the bud/flower will dry quicker. Remember to remove all leaves and separate sugar leaves (sugar leaves) are the leaves tightly wrapped around the bud/flower. You will need some slender scissors for this process. It will be easier to cut the smaller leaves with smaller scissors.

Method 2

Clothes rack; as in method 1 you will need twine and to trim the smaller branches from larger branches. String the stems up on the rack about an inch and a half apart. It can take up to 5 to 6 day to dry efficiently don't rush it. If not dry it will mold in the mason jar. Don't forget they should have no leaves on the stem or around the flower/bud. In both these methods the stems will dry up. The stems will still be green and the very thin stems are sweet. So sweet that you can chew on them. They taste like sweet sticks.

Method 3

This method does not require twine but a nice amount of brown paper bag. Good old fashion brown paper bags. I usually stock up from the market. In this method you cut the bud off the stem. You place the bud in a brown bag and close it The dry time for this can vary from 5to 7 day.

Be mindful you can not fill the brown bag up, only cover the bottom of the bag. Shake the bag every day to promote air movement. You will fold the bag keep in a cool dark until it is dry.

Hemp

Hemp is developed by drying out the root of your plant. Once you have completed you harvest of all the bud/flower that was growing wet the ground and pull the remaining plant out. Pull close to the ground to pull up the root. Wetting the ground makes it a little easier to dig up the ground. Once you up root the plant you will detach the roots. After you cut the root off soak the root in water to clean and debug them. I recommend at least twenty four hours to at least a half an hour. Once you cleaned them let them dry out. They need to dry out in the sun or window no water or moisture this too will mold. Once dried you will skin and crush it using a coulder or a food processor. Once grinded to powder it can be infused in all types of things. When infused into olive oil or coconut butter and or shea butter it becomes a topical aid. This can medically help with pain and rashes etc..

Chapter 6: The Curing State

Curing Stage 1

This is when your mason jars come into play. Place your dry flower into mason jars. Jelly jars and pickle jars are not good to use. Once you break the seal suction on a jelly jar is broken and won't reseal correctly. Pickle jars no matter how long you soak them even with bleach the pickle smell will come back and make your bud smell like pickles. Not good, believe me. Molding smells like vinegar so pickle jars are very very bad. Once you put your bud in jars only fill it halfway to allow for air and space. You must open the jar every day and shake up the bud in the jar to circulate air around the jar You have to open the everyday for ten days. If the bud seems extra moist leave the jar open for an hour or two to allow air to help dry it out without molding. For the first week or two the bud will remain bright green to rich green depending on what color it was when first put in the jar.

The bud will also draw up into itself becoming tighter in formation. This

is normal.

Curing Stage 2

At this stage taste the green. Take a bud/flower and roll it or put it in the hookah. Just a taste, dont go crazy. You still have some curing time to go.Your bud/flower can mature in potency for up to three months. Only two weeks has passed so far so chill. You can easily go through your bud. You want to allow it to mature to its most potent state.

At this point you now will open your mason jars once a week. Now if it is a crazy humid hot day check your jars. You might need to open each one and check its moisture. Mold hits fast and can't be fixed. At least it's not safe to smoke or eat mold spores or modded bud. So check out the jars and open regularly. It's better safe than sorry, trust! Your bud will shrink in size yet the potency of the bud will increase. Keep it out of the sun. You will need to do this for the next four to five weeks.

Curing Stage 3

You made it! Every jar should have an awesomely potent smell and if you haven't smoked through it you now will open the jars once a month. If it is hot where you live check on your bud/flowers and make sure you are shaking it to circulate the air. You bud has also slightly changed in color. The green will be a little duller. The color on the pistols will look a little more brownish red then orangy-red. It also will be a bit more firm aka crunchy.

At this time enjoy what you have grown and created. It's yours, chemically free. If possible slow stroll and enjoy. Your goal should be to get to six month of curing or a least one jar past six months. It will blow your mind. Curing the leaves will make them smooth and smoke like bud.

You should always store your jars in a cool dry place. Checking them periodically to make sure they don't get moist over time.

Chapter 7: Hemp, Butter, Cookies and Dressing

Decarbing:

Decarbing of the bud / flower or leaves, which is basically heating the bud or flower or leaves to activate the THC and turn it into THC acid. Decarbing of the bud helps it to bond to fats easier such as butter or oil. It's believed that when you slow cook the bud without decarb it is not fully activated. Some just use the bud without decarb. They infuse it with butter or oil in a mason jar slow cooked. It has the same effect and happens to taste better. But if you want to decarb the bud / flower this is how

Warning aroma will fill up your house

Foil or parchment paper

Ounce of bud or 2 ounces of leaves * leaves must be grinded*

Grinder

Cookie sheet

Do not grind bud. Only grind leaves if using leaves only grind bud if pairing with leaves. Place bud and or leaves on cookie sheet lined with foil or parchment. Set the oven temperature to 240 degrees F. Make sure to spread into a thin even layer. Do Not over -fill tray. Over filling will result in uneven process. Roast for about 45 minutes. Be very mindful of cooking the product. It can burn fast and ruin. After roasting, let pan cool in oven until pan is cool to the touch. Use product for butter. It should come out golden or a darker green.

Recipes

Cannabutter

Ingredients

-unsalted butter 3-4 ounces /coconut oil Raw

-mason jar

-pot

-cheese cloth

-2 ounce of sugar leaves or 1.5 ounce of flower(bud)

-water

-strainer

Directions

Place bud or leaves in cheese cloth and secure with a tie. Place cheesecloth in mason jar. Place butter in mason jar and squeeze it in. Put water in the pot then sit the strainer in the pot. Make sure the strainer is not sitting directly on the bottom of the pot. Sit the mason jar in the strainer half way filled with water. Let the water come to a boil then let it simmer for four hours. Replace the water as it evaporates. After four hours turn the water off. User clamps or pot holder to remove jar. Pull out cheesecloth and squeeze cheese cloth over the mason jar. Squeeze all excess oil out of the bud. You could use a strainer if its too hot for you to squeeze use a spoon to press against the strainer. What you have in your jar is cannabutter. Butter is made with cream and should be refrigerated. If you want to make with coconut oil use raw coconut oil and follow the same instructions. Coconut oil do not need to be in fridge.

Yum Yum Brownies:

Ingredients:
-1 cup of flour
-1 ⅔ of cocoa powder
-1 cup of cannabutter

-2 eggs

-1 teaspoon of vanilla extract

-2 cups of sugar

-½ cup of almonds (optional)

Brownie pan

Directions:

Preheat oven at 325 f. Blend all dry ingredients together in a bowl. In a separate bowl blend eggs cannabutter and vanilla. Make sure to blend well. Then gradually add wet ingredients to dry ingredients. Blend well then pour in 8x8 pan lined with parchment paper or non stick spray oil. Bake for 40-45 minutes or until fork comes out clean. When done remove from oven let cool and cut and serve * Small pieces are recommended.*

Sunshine Lemon Cookies:

Ingredients:

2 cups of flour

½ teaspoon of baking soda

½ teaspoon of salt

1 tablespoon or more of lemon zest

½ cup of lemon juice

1 cup of sugar

1 large egg

1 teaspoon of vanilla

½ cup of cannabutter

Directions:

Preheat oven at 350
Blend eggs, lemon juice, vanilla extract and sugar together first. In another bowl blend then rest of the ingredients together well. Slowly add wet ingredients to the dry and blend well. Scoop out spoon full of cookie to a parchment lined cookie sheet and bake for 8 to 11 minutes. * The blend will look green its okay it will look like lemon cookies when baked*

Rubble Ranch Dressing:

Ingredients:
½ cup of sour cream

½ cream cheese

1 tablespoon of basil

1 teaspoon of chives

1 teaspoon of parsley

1 teaspoon of dill

1 teaspoon of cannabutter

½ teaspoon garlic powder

½ teaspoon of pepper corn

½ teaspoon of seasalt

Whip together in a bowl until smooth. Chill in refrigerate for a hour or two covered in a bowl. Then it's ready to eat.

Jamming Ginger Cookies:

Ingredients:

1 cup of sugar

1 large egg

¼ cup of molasses

2 ¼ cup of flour

¾ cup of cannabutter

2 tablespoons of powder ginger

1 teaspoon of baking soda

¾ tablespoon of cinnamon

½ teaspoon of powder cloves

¼ teaspoon of salt.

Directions:
Preheat oven 350f Mix eggs, molasses and cannabutter together in a bowl until smooth. Add mixed dry ingredients to the wet ingredients in the bowl and blend well. Scoop out cookie using a spoon. Place on parchment lined cookie sheet and bake for 8 to 11 minutes.

You now own a complete guide to how to grow chemical free cannabis /Bud/ Weed. What every you call it. Your bud has medical properties that are not overshadowed by chemicals. I want to thank everyone for taking the time to reads and use this book as you see fit.

This book was originally written by Magdalene Beckett. It has been inbellished by the publisher Andrea Spruill and Edited by A. C. In Honor of My Mother Ruby Beckett My twin and My boys.

About the Author of this book, Magdalene Beckett is referred to as one of the Monarchs of her family. She survived the south and Migrated to the North to begin a new life. Magdalene was a fighter of hatred and through her agriculture skills feed a community of children. While passing on Tradition she taught her own how to do the same. She left journals documenting her struggles and her growth. Among those journals was one of medicine. She wrote how to grow chemically free Marijuana. We honor her by letting her skills of agriculture live on in this book.